Drums, Rattles, and Bells

written and illustrated
by Larry Kettelkamp

WILLIAM MORROW &
COMPANY 1960

Grateful recognition is given to Professor George Hunter, School of Music, University of Illinois, Urbana, Illinois, for his helpful suggestions.

8   9   10   75

Strike, Shake, and Scrape

We live in a world of sounds. Early men must have noticed many sounds that pleased them—the crack of dry sticks striking each other, the rattle of loose seeds inside a dried gourd, the scrape of a cutting tool drawn across a bumpy surface. Some of the sounds, like the sharp blow of a stone chipping a flint tool, were a part of everyday work. These sounds of striking, shaking, or scraping are called percussion.

3

When men first began using the skins of animals for clothing and shields—which looked much like drums without sides—they softened the skins by soaking them in water, then stretched them on frames. As the skin dried, it shrank. Many early hunters must have noticed that a stretched skin drying on a frame produced a soft, pleasing sound when it was struck.

From all these materials—sticks, stones, seeds, animal skins, and many others—came the percussion instruments used today. Some seem to have no definite pitch. Others, such as the xylophone, can be used to play chords and melodies. Yet all are played by striking, shaking, or scraping.

This book tells you how this important family of instruments, including drums, rattles, and bells, came to be. You will learn how their sounds are produced and how to make and play many of them.

The First Noisemakers

One of the first percussion instruments was the rattle. In a rattle the sound is made by several small, hard objects striking each other or some other material. Rattles were first made of shells or seeds—strung along a cord or tied in bunches. These rattles were fastened to the arms, legs, waist, or neck of a dancer, so that his quick body movements produced noises.

Later rattles were often made of gourds. If you hold a dried gourd by the neck and shake it, the loose seeds inside will make a soft noise. The gourd rattle will produce a louder sound if it is partly filled with pebbles.

6

Cuban gourd scraper

Maracas, a pair of shot-filled gourds with handles attached to them, are used today in Latin-American music. One gourd is held in each hand, handles down. They are shaken alternately, with a flick of the wrist and forearm. The sound is soft and pitchless, but the rhythm is clear.

maracas

Another early noisemaker was the scraper, also used today in Latin-American music. Ridges are cut along one side of a long hollow gourd, and several holes are cut in the other side. The ridges are scraped back and forth with a stick, producing a drawn-out, pitchless sound. The thin, hard wall of the gourd, and the air inside it, reinforce the sound so that it is loud and clear.

Another primitive instrument was nothing more than two sticks struck sharply together. These sticks, used today in Latin-American rhythms, are called claves. They are usually made of hickory wood about six or eight inches long. When this instrument is played, one stick rests lightly on the base of the thumb and fingernails of the left hand, which is made into a fist. The second stick, held lightly in the right hand, strikes the first with a sharp, bouncing stroke.

These three instruments—shakers, scrapers, and sticks—still make music for dances, as they did when they were first developed.

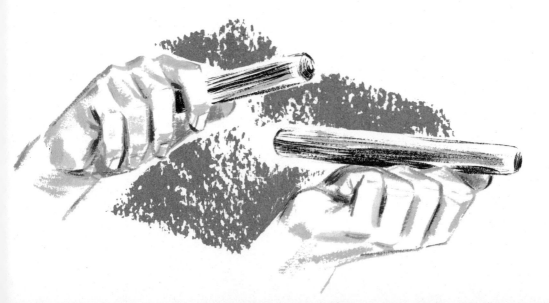

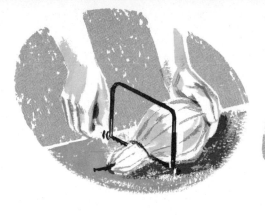

Making Rattles

If you live in a warm area where gourds grow, you can make a rattle easily. First, saw off the neck of a gourd. Bend a stiff wire to the shape shown on page 10, and scrape out the seeds and the pith. Poke a smaller hole in the blossom end. Let the gourd dry completely, and then put a teaspoonful of BB shot or pebbles into it. Whittle a stick or a piece of a wooden dowel to the shape shown on page 10. Insert the stick in the gourd, making sure that the stick fits tightly into the holes. Wrap a string around the part of the stick that passes through the smaller hole. Tie the string tightly and glue it to the stick to prevent the gourd from sliding.

The gourd rattle can now be decorated with water colors or poster paints. After the paint is dry, give the gourd a coat of clear shellac to protect the paint.

Besides gourds, many other materials can be used for making rattles. Baking-powder cans and cylinder-shaped ice-cream cartons will work well. Whittle a stick for any of these containers and finish the construction just as you would for a gourd rattle. Shot, rice, corn, or pebbles can be used as the filler. Use your imagination and experiment with different kinds and amounts of filler to get the sound you like.

bent wire

tie and glue

pebbles or shot

Drums

Many hollow materials give pleasant sounds when they are struck. A section of bamboo or the rotted trunk of a fallen tree are natural hollow objects, and some of the earliest drums were made from such materials.

A section of bamboo, open at the top and closed at the bottom by one of the joints which grow inside it, will produce a hollow sound with a definite pitch if the bottom is struck sharply on the ground. (You can get a similar effect by using a mailing tube with a metal cap on the bottom.) The pitch depends on the length of the tube—the shorter the section of tube, the higher the pitch.

This bamboo section, called a stamping tube, was one of the earliest drums. Today stamping tubes are still played on some of the Pacific islands. A group of women or

11

stamping tube

girls sit in a semicircle on the ground. The players hold a tube in each hand by a handle carved at the top. Tubes of many different sizes are used, so that they produce an organlike sound as they are rhythmically struck on the ground.

Another early drum was made of part of a tree trunk hollowed out through a long narrow slit in its side. The ends of the trunk were solid, and the only opening was the long slit.

At first these slit drums were quite large, but gradually they were made smaller until some could be carried around easily. Today a small double slit drum, called a wood block, is used in both Latin-American dance bands and in orchestras. It is struck sharply with a stick near the edge of either slit. This is the instrument used in the musical poem *Rodeo* by Aaron Copeland to suggest the rhythm of horses' hoofs.

True drums, which have been used by people in every part of the world, are made of animal skin stretched tightly over a shell or container to strengthen the sound. Some drums are deep, some shallow; some have skins stretched over both ends of vase- or bowl-shaped containers. Materials range from hollow tree trunks to shells and bowls made of metal and pottery.

log slit drums

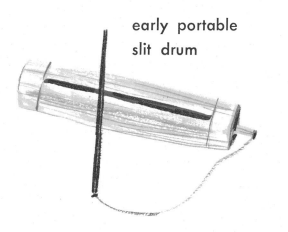

early portable
slit drum

wood block

The bass drum, snare drum, and kettle-drum of today were first used for military music before they became an important part of the orchestra. The snare drum and bass drum are still the core of the military band, in which they sound the beat of marching feet even when no other instruments are playing. When soldiers rode horses, a set of kettledrums were sometimes used, one slung at either side of the player riding the horse.

Kettledrums, also called timpani, are of great importance to the modern orchestra. They are made of calfskin stretched over large copper bowls. The drumheads are struck with felt- or wool-covered sticks.

hourglass drum

Indian hand drum
and barrel drum

footed drum

Timpani can be tuned to clear and definite pitches, and they can be played softer or louder than any other instrument in the orchestra. At first two drums were usually used, one tuned to the basic note of a piece and the other to the fifth tone of the scale in which the piece was written. A German kettledrum player named Ernst Pfundt invented a mechanism with which a foot pedal could be lowered or raised to tighten or loosen the timpani head so that

15

vessel drum

hand-tuned
timpani

modern-pedal
timpani

the pitch could be quickly changed. His invention used heavy weights to balance the pull of the stretched skin. In the last fifty years many changes have been made to simplify the mechanism, and the timpani have become versatile instruments. One drum can sound five notes of a scale and the half steps in between. A drum with a head twenty-eight inches in diameter and another with a twenty-five-inch head can be used together to play a range of over one octave, which is quite remarkable for two drums.

The modern timpanist must have a fine sense of pitch, since he is constantly retuning his drums during the course of a piece. His sense of rhythm must be accurate, for his instrument often provides a foundation for the rest of the orchestra. He must also be highly skilled in order to play the solo passages now written for his drums.

In contrast to the kettledrum, the snare drum is double-headed and is played with two hickory sticks. The top head is called the batter head. The lower is called the snare head, because several strings of gut (called snares) are stretched across it. When these touch the head they vibrate against it as the upper head is struck. The snare head gives the drum its crisp and pitchless sound. In Ravel's *Bolero* the rhythm of the snare drum runs through the entire composition.

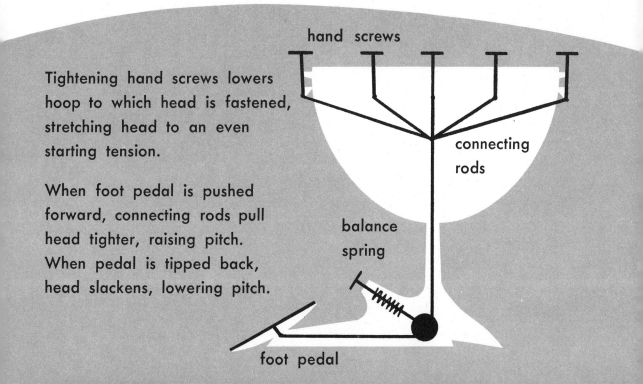

hand screws

Tightening hand screws lowers hoop to which head is fastened, stretching head to an even starting tension.

When foot pedal is pushed forward, connecting rods pull head tighter, raising pitch. When pedal is tipped back, head slackens, lowering pitch.

connecting rods

balance spring

foot pedal

The drum can also be played without the snare effect. Then it sounds a more definite pitch, though it is not as clear as that of the kettledrum. The snare drum is also used as a jazz instrument. Here it is often played with wire brushes so that the accents it makes are softer.

The bass drum, which is also double-headed, is much larger than the snare drum. It is struck with a felt or lamb's-wool beater held in the hand. The sound is low and muffled, but the drum can be played quite loudly. In jazz bands the bass drum is played with a foot pedal, leaving the hands free to play the snare drum or some other percussion instrument.

jazz percussion outfit

Several drums are used especially for the rhythms of Latin-American dance music. The largest is the congo drum. This drum, whose length is much greater than its width, is covered at only one end and tapers so that it is slightly smaller at the open end. It is played only with the hands. Bongo drums are smaller and not as deep. Often a player uses a pair of different sizes, the smaller one having a higher pitch. They are usually held between the knees and are struck with the hands, much like the larger congo drum.

bongo drums

The tambourine is a shallow drum covered with a single calfskin head. Metal jingles are spaced around the wooden shell. The drumhead can be struck with the knuckles or against the knee. The sound of the jingles is added to the rhythm played on the drumhead. Sometimes the instrument is shaken so that only the jingles sound. The tambourine is associated with Spain and is used as an accompaniment for the swirling skirts and stamping feet of Spanish dances.

Building Drums

If there is a music store in your town, you can probably get some used drumheads for nothing more than the time taken to ask for them. A used kettledrum or bass drumhead can supply enough skin for 3 or 4 smaller drums. If no used drumheads are available, a full-sized oatmeal box can be used with or without the lid as a single or double-headed drum. You can also cut up an old inner tube and use it as a substitute for covering material.

A drum can be made out of almost any container that is cylinder- or bowl-shaped and strong enough to support the pull of the skin stretched over one or both ends. Here are the steps in building a simple double-headed drum.

First, get an empty 2-pound coffee can. Remove the bottom of the can with a can opener, then use a pair of pliers to turn down the sharp edge left inside the rim.

22

Punch several holes in the side of the can with a hammer and nail.

With a pencil compass draw 2 circles, 7½ inches in diameter, on the old drumhead. Push the point of the compass into a small piece of cardboard or wood so that it will not pierce the skin. Cut out the 2 circles with a pair of scissors. With pencil and ruler divide each circle into 8 pie shapes. Use a paper punch to make a hole on each pencil line, about ½ inch from the edge of the circle.

Next you will need a long, narrow strip of skin to fasten the two drumheads together. Simply cut around the edge of the large used drumhead, making the strip of

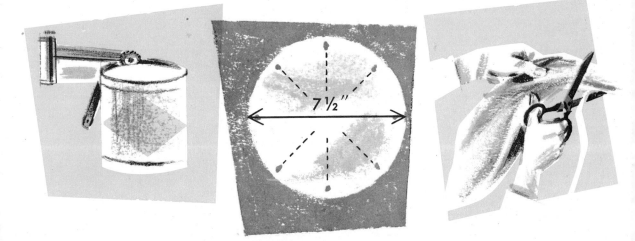

skin about ¼ inch wide. Keep cutting until you have a strip about 6 feet long. Next, soak the skins and the thong in cool water for a half hour to make them soft and flexible.

Place one drumhead on the table, the can on top of it, and the second drumhead on top of the can. Use the thong to lace the 2 heads together through the punched holes, just as you would lace up your shoes. Pull the thong just tight enough so that it is not slack, and tie the 2 ends together with a square knot. The skin will shrink as it dries, and within 2 or 3 hours the drum will be ready to play.

If you want to paint a design on your

drum, you can do so in 2 steps. Before you attach the drumheads, paint the coffee can a basic color with an oil-base paint, being sure that you clean your brush in turpentine, paint thinner, or paint solvent. Some of the new spray paints are also easy to use. Let the paint dry thoroughly. After you have laced on the water-soaked drumheads, you can paint on them while they are still damp. Use water colors or poster paints just as you would on a piece of paper. After the heads are dry, the paint will not come off. Bird and animal silhouettes, star shapes and other geometric patterns, can be used to decorate the drum. Keep the design simple. The drawings of drums in this book may give you ideas for other designs.

25

If you have an old wooden mixing bowl, you can make a one-headed drum by fastening the wet skin over the rim of the container with carpet tacks spaced about an inch apart. Use a wood auger to drill several good-sized holes in the bottom of the bowl. They will let air enter and leave the bowl as the head vibrates. Once you have learned to soak, lace, and tack drumheads, you are limited only by the sizes and kinds of materials you can find for drum shells.

Some drums sound well when struck with the finger tips; others sound well with narrow sticks. To make a beater you can use a small rubber ball and a Tinkertoy stick or wooden dowel rod. Work a hole part way into the ball with an ice pick, handling the pick carefully. Force the end of the stick into the hole. If you want to soften the sound of the beater, fold a small piece of toweling over the ball and tie it to the stick.

26

Keyboard Percussion

The sounds of both wood and metal are used in the keyboard instruments of the percussion family. Sometimes the keyboard looks like that of a piano. Pressing a key works a mechanism that strikes a bar of metal. On others, the bars themselves are arranged like piano keys and struck with mallets.

The xylophone was the earliest keyboard percussion instrument. *Xylon* means *wood* and *phone* means *sound,* so the word *xylophone* means *sound of wood.* The first xylophones were slabs of wood of different lengths placed across the player's legs as he sat on the ground. The instrument was improved by laying the boards across two logs instead of the legs of the player.

If slabs of wood are of the same width

and thickness, the shorter slabs will give higher pitches. Thus wood can be cut to produce the exact tones the player wishes. A vibrating bar of wood has two nodes, or spots, where it does not vibrate. If the bar is struck at a node, the tone sounds dead. Because of this, the bars of a xylophone are supported at these two nodes.

With granulated soap powder you can find the nodes of a bar of wood. Place the bar on a level surface and sprinkle the powder along the entire length of the wood. Strike the wood near the center with a stick or hammer. The powder will start to jump around. Gradually, some will be shaken off the wood, and that which remains will move to two small areas of the block. These areas are the nodes—where there is little or no vibration.

On some early xylophones hollow gourds of various sizes were placed beneath the bars. If a gourd was the correct size, the

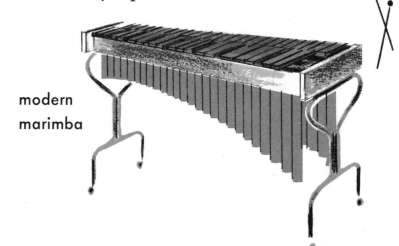

xylophone with gourd resonators

air inside would vibrate at the same pitch as the key and strengthen the sound. It was also found that if the wooden bars were thinner in the center than near the ends, the tone would be better.

Today musicians use an instrument called a marimba, which is made of rosewood bars placed over resonating tubes closed at one end. The sound is mellow, since the resonators reinforce the basic pitch, or fundamental, of each bar and reduce the overtones.

The modern xylophone has bars like

modern marimba

those of the marimba, and they are struck with plastic or rubber mallets. It has no resonators. The sound of the wood is sharp, with brilliant overtones. The composer Saint-Saëns used the xylophone in *Danse Macabre* (dance of death) to represent the sound of skeletons dancing about in a graveyard.

When men learned to make metals, they found that bars of metal could be struck to give pleasing sounds. In Java an instrument called the saron was made of bronze bars placed over a wooden sounding box. The glockenspiel used today is much like the saron, except that the bars are now made of steel or aluminum. When used in a marching band, the glockenspiel is sometimes called the bell-lyra. In the

modern
xylophone

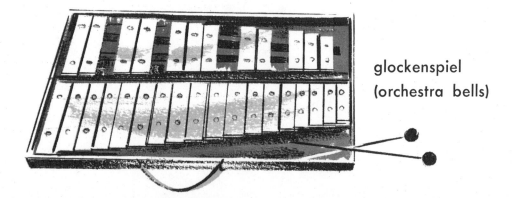

glockenspiel
(orchestra bells)

orchestra it is often called the orchestra bells. The bars are struck with a hard rubber mallet, and the tones are brilliant and bell-like.

Another Javanese instrument, called the gender, used sections of bamboo beneath bronze keys to strengthen the sounds. The vibraphone, popular today in both orchestras and dance bands, has resonating tubes of aluminum to reinforce the sounds of the steel or aluminum keys.

A variation of these instruments is the celesta, which has a keyboard like that of a piano. When a key is pressed, a felt-covered hammer strikes the center of a metal bar. The sound is like that of the glockenspiel, except that metal resonating tubes make the sound more mellow. In

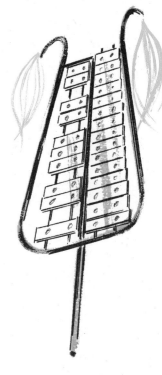

bell lyra

On the vibraphone an electric motor spins discs inside the resonators to add a tremolo to the tones. Foot pedal works felt dampers, which can stop bars from sounding.

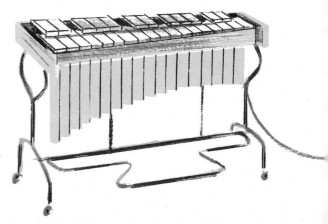

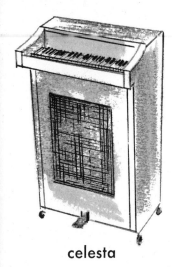

celesta

Tchaikovsky's *Nutcracker Suite,* the *Dance of the Sugar Plum Fairy* is played on the celesta.

The melodies and chords which can be played on the xylophone, marimba, vibraphone, glockenspiel, and celesta make the percussion family a versatile group indeed.

Building a Xylophone

With some wood and corrugated cardboard you can make a xylophone which you can tune to play a complete scale of eight notes—do, re, mi, fa, sol, la, ti, do. The best wood for xylophones is rosewood, but almost any wood will give some tone, and any hardwood—such as walnut—will work well. The xylophone on page 34 has bars made of wood 1 inch thick and 2 inches wide. Bars cut to the lengths marked on page 33 will almost have the right pitches, but they will have to be tuned. To raise the pitch, saw a little wood off

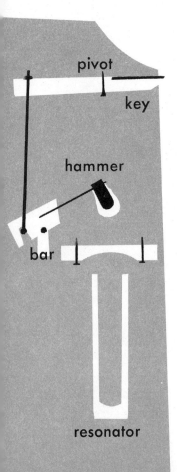

pivot

key

hammer

bar

resonator

32

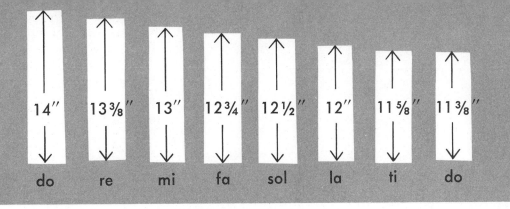

14"	13⅜"	13"	12¾"	12½"	12"	11⅝"	11⅜"
do	re	mi	fa	sol	la	ti	do

the end of the bar. To lower the pitch, plane off some of the surface of the bar to make it thinner. It is easier to tune the scale by sawing the ends of the bars.

You can test the tone of a bar by holding it at one end, about two inches from the top, between your thumb and first finger. Let it hang loosely as you tap it near the center with a hammer. If the wood has a flaw, such as a knot or a split, the tone may be dead, and you will have to saw a new bar. If your ear is good, you may be able to tune the bars just by listening. If you have a piano, you can tune the bars to a major scale—do, re, mi, fa, sol, la, ti, do. Simply shorten the bars until they match the nearest piano pitches.

33

The bars are placed over a box made of corrugated cardboard. If you use the measurements given in the drawing, the edges of the box will support the bars near their nodes. A good mallet for striking can be made of a stick and a wooden knob from a Tinkertoy set. Fasten a piece of a towel around the wooden knob with a rubber band.

Strike the bars near the center for the best tone. With a little practice you will be able to play many tunes on your xylophone.

Bells

From the tinkle of a cowbell to the powerful ring of the largest church bells, bell music is fascinating. Bells have been symbols of magic and religion, they mark the hours of the day, they announce important events, and they ring both in mourning and for occasions of great joy. Bell music is penetrating, and the sound of large bells can be heard many miles away.

Bells are usually made of brass—a mixture of tin and copper. They are cup-shaped. They are struck at the rim of the large open end and do not sound at the smaller closed end. The basic pitch, or fundamental, is often weak compared with the strong overtones, and so the bell has

St. Mark's Cathedral and bell tower in Venice, Italy

a mysterious and sometimes pitchless sound. Bells can be made as finely as other instruments, however. They can be carefully tuned so that they are capable of playing music of great beauty.

Bells are a part of the tradition of Christianity. In Rome, in the early days of Christianity, the churches used bells to announce the time of meeting. Then larger bells were placed in towers above the churches, so that the ringing could be heard for great distances. Use of church bells spread to England and then to other European countries.

Bells are also important in Oriental countries. In both China and Japan bells are placed in the temples. Large Japanese temple bells are struck from the outside with a tree trunk rather than with a clapper on the inside. The trunk hangs on chains, parallel to the ground. Many men pull back the trunk, and when they release

town crier

Japanese
temple bell

it, the trunk's end swings against the bell.

In the Netherlands and Belgium, single bells were placed in watchtowers. Gradually more bells of various sizes were added, until complete musical scales could be played on them, with one bell for each note. These sets of bells were called carillons. Fine musicians became interested in the bells and learned to play them. Churches had carillons made for their towers. Some of these instruments are now hundreds of years old and still sound as they did when first made.

Today huge carillons can be found in many of the large cities of the world.

Those in the Riverside Church in New York and in the University of Chicago chapel have over seventy bells. The largest bell in the Riverside Church weighs about eighteen tons.

Carillon music is written like piano or organ music, and the bells are played with a special keyboard. The player uses felt pads to protect his fingers, so he can play for long periods of time. With his fists and feet he strikes wooden levers with a strong bouncing motion. Wires connect the levers to clappers placed close to the rim of each bell. The bells are firmly anchored to overhead beams and do not swing. As a clapper strikes a bell, it moves only an inch or two and then is quickly

inside a carillon

pulled back by a coil spring so that the bell can be struck again when needed. To the ears of the carillonneur—as the player is called—the music sounds thunderous and full of clashing overtones, but to listeners outside the tower the music has a beauty matched by no other instrument.

For years hand bells have been used for many purposes. They were rung in the streets of Rome to announce when the

carillon tower of Riverside Church in New York City

early
hand bells

public baths were ready. They were rung to call servants, and in the days when there were few clocks, they were rung by town criers to mark the hours. The postman and the muffin man used bells to announce their coming. Even today the traveling ice-cream vendor rings a bell as he passes through the streets.

Hand-bell ringing has grown in popularity recently. Several English and European companies now cast musical hand bells. These are carefully tuned by grinding away parts of the bells. Grinding the rim to shorten the bell raises the pitch. Grinding the inside to make it wider lowers it.

The hand bell is held upright by a leather handle. A spring inside the bell

holds the clapper a little away from the rim. A gentle flick of the wrist and arm is enough to ring the bell. Hand bells are so carefully tuned that even the chords that are played on a piano can be rung and will sound well.

Hand bells are being bought by churches and other groups. The interest is so new that very little music is available. Each group must make many of its own arrangements for its particular set of bells. However, the American Guild of English Hand-bell Ringers has been formed to standardize hand-bell ringing, and more music should soon be available.

In a hand-bell choir each person handles two or more bells. The group is not com-

clapper

spring

modern
hand bell

triangle

orchestra chimes

plete without every member present. Hand-bell ringing is a great deal of fun even for a group with little musical training. Listening to hand-bell choirs is a new treat which many of us can look forward to.

Since bells must be made very large in order to sound low pitches, the symphony orchestra uses a set of chimes in place of bells. This instrument is easily portable. The chimes are hollow tubes of chrome-plated brass, about one inch wide and from four to six feet long. The chimes are hung inside a large frame. A wooden hammer covered with rawhide is used to strike the chimes at the upper ends, producing a bell-like sound.

The triangle, too, has a tinkling, bell-like tone. It is made of a steel rod bent into a triangular shape. It is hung on a gut string and struck inside with another steel rod. The overtones are so strong that the sound seems pitchless.

In addition to the chimes, the orchestra includes two other instruments with the penetrating sound of brass—the gong and the cymbals. The best gongs come from the Orient. This instrument is made of a circle of brass with a rolled rim. It is hung in a frame and struck with a soft mallet. Unlike the bell, the gong vibrates in the center and is dead at the rim. Its pitchless and strange tone is usually used for special effects.

Cymbals are shaped more like dinner plates than gongs. Usually two cymbals are struck together, held by leather straps fastened to the centers. The jazz musician uses cymbals mounted on a stand, and the cymbals are struck together by pressing a foot pedal.

Bells, chimes, gongs, and cymbals all make use of the mysterious and penetrating sound of brass, and their music is heard and enjoyed everywhere.

Oriental gong

orchestra cymbals

43

Chinese
stone chimes

Building a Water-Glass Carillon

From your own experience you know that many common objects produce bell-like tones. Drinking glasses, crystal glasses, aluminum glasses, bottles, teacups, saucers, and even flowerpots may give pleasant musical sounds when struck. The Chinese discovered that even certain types of stones produced pleasing musical tones. They built chimes of L-shaped stones of different sizes, hung by strings inside an upright frame.

With very little trouble you can make a set of drinking-glass bells. Get a thick bath towel, fold it in half the long way, and spread it flat on a table top. This will cushion the glasses so that nothing will interfere with the tones. With 5 glasses of a single size, you can tune the first 5 tones of a major scale—do, re, me, fa, sol. Strike all 5 glasses to find the one with the highest pitch and the one with the lowest pitch.

Place the highest-toned glass at the right-hand end of the towel and the lowest-toned one at the left. Space the other 3 glasses in a row in between, with all glasses upright. Strike the glass on the right and sing sol on the pitch it gives. Then sing backwards down the scale—sol, fa, mi, re, do. Keep humming the note for do. Slowly pour water into the glass at the left. As you add water the pitch will get lower. Keep filling the glass until the pitch matches the note you are singing. You will probably need to fill the glass about 2/3 or 3/4 full to get the tone low enough. Tune the 3 in-between glasses with water in the same way, matching them to re, mi, and fa.

Like a true bell, a glass vibrates near the rim and is dead at the closed bottom. To strike the glasses, hold a pencil or other stick near one end so that it hangs loosely between your thumb and first finger. Let

45

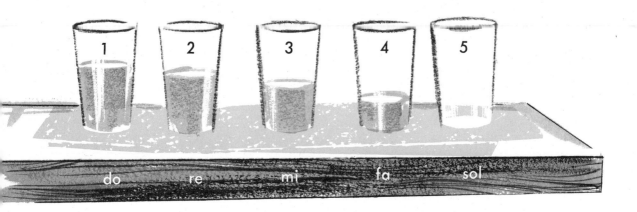

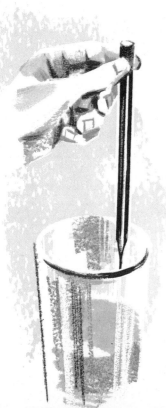

the free end of the stick swing gently
against the outside of the rim of the glass
so that it bounces away and lets the glass
keep ringing.

Here is a tune you can try with 5 glasses.
Number the glasses 1 to 5 from left to
right. Strike the glasses like this: 3 2 1 2
3 3 3 (pause) 2 2 2 (pause) 3 5 5 (pause)
3 2 1 2 3 3 3 3 2 2 3 2 1. If you do this
correctly, you will play *Mary Had a Little
Lamb*.

To produce a continuous tone, swing
the stick back and forth just inside the
glass, letting it strike first one side and
then the other. Use a stick in each hand
when you play the song this way, and al-

ternate hands as you switch from glass to glass, to make the tones connect smoothly.

You may be able to get surprising sounds from your water-glass carillon and from your homemade xylophone, drums, and rattles. Perhaps you can follow up these experiments by playing and listening to some of the real percussion instruments. You may not become an expert musician, but when you know how the sounds are produced, you can recognize and enjoy them in the music you hear.

No other family has such a wide variety of instruments as the percussion family. They were probably the first musical instruments made by man and are still an important part of music everywhere.

Musical Terms

chord two or more notes sounded together

fundamental basic pitch of a tone, usually the lowest and loudest

jazz improvised music that stresses offbeat accents, usually played against 2- or 4-beat rhythms and chord patterns of well-known songs

note sign indicating fixed pitch of a tone and its duration

octave interval of 12 half steps separating two notes with the same name

overtones pitches higher than the fundamental that also form part of a musical tone; number and strength of the overtones determine the tone color of an instrument or voice

pitch the level of a tone, measured in number of vibrations per second

resonator device which vibrates with the original sound source on the same pitch and amplifies the sound

rhythm time or beat in music; also a pattern of long and short notes

scale a series of successive tones starting and ending with *do*

sol-fa syllables do, re, mi, fa, sol, la, ti, do One example is the tones sounded by the keys C D E F G A B C on a piano.

vibration fast, regular, back-and-forth movement